Montana's

UPPER MISSOURI RIVER BREAKS
NATIONAL MONUMENT

TEXT AND PHOTOS BY RICK AND SUSIE GRAETZ

The Montana Series

NUMBER SEVEN

This book was produced in partnership with the River and Plains Society of Fort Benton, Montana, the governing board for the Upper Missouri Museum, and the Montana Agricultural Center and Museum of the Northern Great Plains.

The authors thank the staff of the Bureau of Land Management's Lewistown Field Office for their assistance with the project.

PHOTOGRAPHY CONTRIBUTIONS BY:

Erwin and Peggy Bauer ▪ Chuck Haney ▪ Larry Mayer ▪ Wayne Mumford
Karen Nichols ▪ Donnie Sexton/Travel Montana ▪ George Wuerthner ▪ Russell Young

©2001 Northern Rockies Publishing
Rick and Susie Graetz
P.O. Box 1707, Helena, Montana 59624
norockpub@aol.com

Design by GingerBee
gingerbee@qwest.net

All color, design and prepress work done in Montana, U.S.A.
Printed in Korea
ISBN 1-891152-10-6

Front Cover:
Near Dark Butte (mile 69.5).
KAREN NICHOLS

Back Cover:
A modern day Corps of Discovery explores
the Lewis and Clark campsite of May 31, 1805.
RICK AND SUSIE GRAETZ

Prairie falcons are
counted among the
230 types of birds
found within the
National Monument.
ERWIN AND PEGGY BAUER

Feeling insignificant.
At mile 54, two miles
below Pilot Rock.
RUSSELL YOUNG

Chouteau
County
Courthouse,
built in 1884.
RICK AND SUSIE GRAETZ

FORT BENTON

MONTANA'S BIRTHPLACE – RIVER MILE 0

—))()

High on a sandstone bluff north of town, spotters once sighted steamboats chugging upriver eight miles away. Word then went out to the townsfolk that a steamboat was "round the bend!" Today from this Signal Point, there's a great view of the big Missouri, historic Fort Benton, the Bear's Paw Mountains to the northeast and the Highwood Mountains in the southeast.

The Corps of Discovery led by Captains Lewis and Clark passed by the future site of Fort Benton on June 13, 1805 after having camped about eight miles downstream.

In 1845, Alexander Culbertson of the American Fur Company established Fort Lewis, a trading post just upstream and on the opposite bank from today's Fort Benton. When the Blackfeet tribe complained that ice jams and floods made it difficult for them to reach it in the winter and spring, Culbertson agreed to move the post. In the spring of 1847, structures were dismantled and the logs floated to the new site three miles downriver on the south bank. The new post carried the Fort Lewis name at first, then later was changed to Fort Clay. With the arrival of the first residents that spring of '47, the oldest continuing settlement in the state came to life.

On Christmas night in 1850, Culbertson announced the name of the fort and village would be formally changed to Fort Benton, in honor of US Senator Thomas Hart Benton, a patron of the American Fur Company.

The population grew and Fort Benton soon became a boisterous "old west" town of legend. As Winfield Stocking wrote, "Although it continued to be a mere village in size, in a commercial way it was the Chicago of the plains. It was the door through which all the gold hunters, adventurers, speculators, traders, land-seekers, big game hunters, fugitives from justice, desperadoes and all the bad Indians on the top of the earth entered the Northwest." A sign on the levee states that the street along the river was "The bloodiest block in the west."

The initial economy was driven by the extremely lucrative fur trade. Before steamboats, heavily loaded 60-foot long, flat-bottomed mackinaws and 70-foot long keel boats were used to transport furs downriver to "the states." When this business began to dwindle, the Missouri River Steamboat Era (1859–1888) brought new life to the community.

On May 28, 1859, the Spread Eagle and the Chippewa left St. Louis. The goal of these mountain boats, as the river men called them, was to make the 2,385-mile upriver journey to Fort Benton. On July 17, 1859, the Chippewa came within 14 miles of its objective when it reached Brulé Bottoms, the site of old Fort McKenzie which had been burned by the Blackfeet in 1843. The fuel supply was depleted and there was no possibility of obtaining more without retreating a great distance. At the same time, the water level of the river was declining, so the freight was unloaded and on July 19 the steamboat headed back downstream.

The next season, the Chippewa and its companion, Key West, tried again. This time luck was on their side and on July 2, 1860, the Chippewa was the first steamboat ever to dock at Fort Benton.

The Key West followed.

Throughout this colorful period, an average of 20 boats per year struggled up the Missouri toward the frontier town. Since close to $50,000 could be grossed from the trip upriver, it was quite a profitable business for the operators, and the downstream excursion paid for itself with passengers and outgoing freight. The trip up to Fort Benton from St.Louis took close to 60 days and cost about $150 a person.

Upriver journeys for the mountain boats were especially dangerous. Shallow and murky waters hid shifting sandbars that changed the channels, treacherous tree snags, called sawyers, lurked just below the water surface and rapids often stalled progress. Then there were the Native Americans who immensely resented these trespassers and instilled fear in the white intruders plying the river. All in all though, through 1888, an estimated 600 steamboats arrived at Fort Benton safely.

Gold discoveries in western Montana created a rush that attracted would-be miners and others to the territory. Missouri steamboats were the most practical mode of transportation; an estimated 10,000 people made the journey, along with countless tons of freight. From the time the ice melted in the spring until the river froze in the fall, Fort Benton's one and one-half-mile long levee was constantly heaped with goods headed for the gold camps of southwest Montana.

Nearly 150 tons of gold, then valued at $75 million (today more than $1 billion), left Montana via the steamboats. The Luella, piloted by Grant Marsh, took the richest cargo ever downriver. Two and one-half tons of gold, then valued at $1,250,000 (at current prices $26,000,000) was on board.

All manners of transportation—freight wagons, stagecoaches, galloping horses as well as an assortment of river craft—were used to advance the steamboat goods to other parts of Montana. But on the land, freight wagons were the mainstay and lifeline in and out of Fort Benton. Moved by the shear strength of oxen, mules or horses, they could transport up to two tons of cargo. Oxen were favored, as Indians had no interest in taking them and they could forage for their own food. Guided by "bullwhackers" who walked along side cracking a whip, these reliable wagons covered from 12 to 15 miles a day.

In those early years, "all trails lead out of Fort Benton" was a familiar statement. The Judith Basin Road headed to Coulson, later to be called Billings. The Barker Road pointed south to the Little Belt Mountains and the Fisk Wagon Road arced up toward the Milk River Country and eventually on to Minnesota. Another historic byway, the Cow Island Trail, a route from one of the steamboat low-water, landing places, went north to just below the Bear Paw Mountains and then turned south meeting the Fisk Wagon Road.

Best known of all the routes were the Whoop Up and Mullan trails. Although it was the first wagon route to cross the Northern Rockies, the roughness of the Mullan Road prevented it from becoming a major thoroughfare. Started in the spring of 1859 near present day Walla Walla, Washington by US Army Captain John Mullan, it meandered east to the Coeur d'Alene Mission in Idaho, then over the Bitterroot Mountains via Look Out Pass reaching St. Regis, Montana in the winter of 1859. Mullan made it to Hellgate, today's Missoula in the spring of 1860. The new "highway" then followed the Clark Fork River and crossed the Continental Divide at present day Mullan Pass dropping down into Helena and on to its completion at Fort Benton on August 1, 1860. When the road was finished, it tied together the heads of navigation for the Missouri and the Columbia rivers.

The steamboat
"DeSmet" at
Fort Benton
ca 1870.
MONTANA HISTORICAL
SOCIETY

▸ The gracious
Grand Union,
built in 1882,
is the oldest
operating hotel
in Montana.
RICK AND SUSIE GRAETZ

Fort Benton was initially meant to be a trading post, not a military fort. However on July 5, 1869, a small detachment of soldiers was assigned to the area, remaining there until June of 1881. The place also served, from 1855 to 1869, as the first Blackfeet Agency.

In September of 1887, the Great Northern Railroad made it to Fort Benton, signaling the beginning of the end for the river trade era; it seemed Fort Benton would die. But the establishment of the Whoop Up Trail opened a trade boom with Canada. This legendary route stretched 240 miles north from Fort Benton through open prairie and river-carved grasslands. Climbing out of the Fort Benton bottoms it followed the Teton River, then after crossing the Marias the new route turned north, passing to the west of the Sweet Grass Hills entering Canada near today's town of Sweet Grass, the trail eventually reached Fort McCloud, a dusty Canadian outpost on the Oldman River, south of Calgary.

This road's best years were from 1874 to 1884. In 1883, when the Canadian Pacific Railroad reached Medicine Hat, Alberta, the trail soon lost its importance. During the Whoop Up Trail's heyday, it supplied Northwest Canadian Mounted Police posts, government sites, Indians and ranchers. As Paul Sharpe stated in his book, *Whoop-Up Country* ". . . it reached into the north, writing its history in whiskey, guns, furs, freight and pioneer enterprise." Today, prairie vegetation has all but obscured most of the old path.

The advent of the railroad in Canada, as well as the extension of railroad lines throughout northern Montana, heralded the end of Fort Benton's boom days. The town never became a rail center as was hoped. After 1888, agriculture needed to be its future. Presently, Fort Benton is the seat of Chouteau County. Named for the Chouteau family, owners of the American Fur Company who brought the first steamboat to town, the county is Montana's top wheat producing region.

The historic bridge that exists today on the levee as a scenic walkway, was erected at a cost of $60,000 and opened in mid-December, 1888. Originally a toll bridge, its main purpose was to ensure Fort Benton would be a primary destination for wool arriving from Meagher County and the Judith Basin. Built in the hope more steamboats would come, a moveable span, destroyed on June 6, 1908 by a rampaging flood, was installed to allow their passage. With the exception of a couple of government work boats, none appeared. The last commercial boat docked here in 1890, and on June 10, 1921, the Mandan, a federally owned craft, came upriver and Fort Benton took its last look at a large vessel.

One of the most fascinating and prettiest towns in Montana to visit, especially when seen in the spring, summer and fall months, Fort Benton embraces its heritage. The cottonwood-lined Missouri River flows peacefully along a well maintained levee area of parks, commercial buildings and old homes. It's hard to imagine that this peaceful agricultural town was as boisterous and raucous as the stories tell. But the sights and sounds of history past are part of what makes Fort Benton so special today. The townsfolk have gone out of their way to preserve important reminders of a way of life that once was.

Remains of the adobe fort buildings, two museums — the Museum of the Northern Great Plains and the Museum of the Upper Missouri, restored homes, a keelboat and the 1888 bridge add to a pleasant walking tour along the levee under massive and stately trees. You can see the firehouse, built in 1883, and learn of the story of "Old Shep" a legendary Fort Benton sheep dog. The Bureau of Land Management maintains a commendable visitor's center. Here you can obtain information on floating the river as well as learning of outfitters and places renting canoes. A couple of blocks in from the riverfront, the county courthouse, built in 1884, is still in use.

Then there is the town's pride and joy, the newly refurbished Grand Union, Montana's oldest operating hotel. This historic landmark was originally opened on November 1, 1882 and constructed in part by more than 500,000 locally fired bricks. As one of the levee signs says, "US Army officers, Canadian Mounties, trappers, miners, traders, river captains, stockman, missionaries, Indian agents and road agents rubbed shoulders in the Grand Union's lobby, spacious dining room and adjourned to its well stocked bar for the relaxation due the frontiersman at a weary journey's end."

Although the hotel operated fairly consistently from 1882 to 1983, it was essentially just a shell when Jim and Cheryl Gagnon bought it and embarked on their dream to restore the building to its former glory, and to preserve as much of the historic value as possible. What a magnificent job they have done.

This is a town that every Montanan should visit at least once. If you were born in Montana, it is part of your inheritance.

▲ Fort Benton levee, 1870.
COURTESY OF JACK LEPLEY

▸▸ In the White Rocks area near Dark Butte.
RICK AND SUSIE GRAETZ

▸ Lewis and Clark's
Decision Point,
the confluence
of the Marias and
Missouri rivers.
WAYNE MUMFORD

Hiking above
Woodhawk
Bottoms
(mile 131).
GEORGE WUERTHNER

THE UPPER MISSOURI RIVER BREAKS NATIONAL MONUMENT

The trickle and rush of water coming from mountain snowmelt, springs and creeks atop the divides of the Bitterroot and Gallatin ranges of southwestern Montana, give birth to the Jefferson, Madison and Gallatin rivers. At Three Forks, these high country waters join to power the initial surge of the fabled Missouri River.

Soon after cutting through "The Gates of the Mountains," the Missouri meets the Montana prairie where it finds room to grow and meander. Other waterways like the Dearborn, Smith, Sun, Teton and Marias join in to further energize "The Big Muddy." As the mighty stream passes Fort Benton, it enters a unique region where it can flow in peace through a magnificent landscape barely touched over time, except by Mother Nature. Here, the river commences its role as the centerpiece of the Upper Missouri River Breaks National Monument and is now protected forever.

No records exist that show how far in 1743 the French Canadian de la Verendrye brothers traveled up the Missouri. Although they were assumed to be the first white men to venture into the Upper Missouri River country, the ultimate historical highlight of the waterway is that of the travelers who came through in 1805 and 1806 . . . Lewis and Clark.

Appointed by President Thomas Jefferson, Meriwether Lewis and William Clark, with their Corps of Discovery, left Camp Dubois near St. Louis, Missouri at 4 PM on May 14, 1804, embarking on one of history's most storied expeditions . . . the investigation of the northern sector of the recently acquired Louisiana Purchase. Specifically, Jefferson's instructions were ". . . the object of your mission is to explore the Missouri River & such principle stream of it, as, by its course and communication with the waters of the Pacific Ocean may offer the most direct & practical water communication across this continent for the purposes of commerce."

The significance of this journey on our nation's history is summed up in the quote by Roy Appleman in his publication written for the National Park Service ". . . they carried the destiny as well as the flag of our young Nation westward, from the Mississippi across thousands of miles of mostly unknown land . . . up the Missouri, over the Rocky Mountains and on to the Pacific. This epic feat not only sparked national pride, but it also fired the imagination of the American people and made them feel for the first time the full sweep of the continent on which they lived."

Prior to their trip, the West was a mysterious place; virgin territory passed through by only a handful of white explorers. Once these two leaders made their journals known, all manners of others followed their lead, most via the Missouri River.

Lewis and Clark were not only brilliant explorers, but also humanitarians. Appleman noted that hostilities with the Native Americans were limited and ". . . were undoubtedly far less severe than they might have been were it not for the reservoir of goodwill the expedition had left with nearly all the western tribes . . . blending fairness, honesty and strength with patience, respect and understanding, Lewis and Clark recognized the personal dignity of the Indians, honored their religion and culture . . . and tried to establish inter-tribal peace. Masters of primitive psychology, they instinctively and unerringly always seemed to make the right decision and rarely offended the natives."

Unfortunately, many of those who came later didn't exhibit the same attitude.

It took nearly a year for the party to reach the confluence of the Missouri and Yellowstone rivers, located in present day North Dakota. On April 27, 1805, after having spent a couple of days at the meeting of these great waters, the Corps entered what eventually would become Montana Territory.

Now setting foot in country they described as more beautiful than could ever have been imagined, Lewis and Clark were particularly impressed with the abundance of wildlife encountered.

The two captains spent four months following the Missouri through eastern and central Montana, past the future sites of Great Falls and Helena to what is now Three Forks, then routing up the Jefferson River to the Beaverhead and its confluence with Red Rock Creek, the site of today's Clark Canyon Reservoir. From there, they traversed west through Horse Creek Prairie to Lemhi Pass arriving on the Continental Divide and the Idaho border on August 12, 1805. One of the farthest headwater trickles of the Missouri had been reached.

Their path then proceeded down the west side of the Divide to Idaho's Lemhi River Valley, continued north to the Salmon River, and led once again back into Montana via what would become Lost Trail Pass. Moving up the Bitterroot Valley to a place they called Travellers Rest near present day Lolo, the Corps turned west again crossing Lolo Pass into Idaho, eventually finding their way to the Pacific Ocean. The journey was now half over.

After spending a miserable, wet and cold winter at Fort Clatsop on the Oregon coast, they retraced their path to Lolo Pass arriving at Travellers Rest on June 29, 1806. It was at this point, the two leaders decided to separate. Lewis headed through present day Missoula, up the Blackfoot River and across today's Lewis and Clark Pass, west of Lincoln. Attaining the Continental Divide at this point, Lewis and his men trekked to the Sun River and ultimately were reunited with the Missouri.

Clark, upon leaving Travellers Rest, again followed part of the previous route down the Bitterroot River then entered the Big Hole Valley on his way to a cache they had left hidden near Horse Creek. Navigating the Beaverhead and Jefferson rivers to Three Forks, he and his men turned east through the Gallatin Valley and on to the Yellowstone River, following it all the way to the Missouri. Clark rejoined Lewis and the Expedition continued to St. Louis, reaching the terminus of their adventure on September 23, 1806.

The Montana landscape Lewis and Clark viewed almost 200 years ago, especially along stretches of the Missouri River from the North Dakota line to Fort Benton, has changed little.

The Corps of Discovery came into what is now The Upper Missouri River Breaks National Monument on May 24, 1805, making camp three miles upstream from today's Fred Robinson Bridge. Pulling boats upriver, sometimes in water to their armpits, and walking through mud, the men toiled mightily to ascend the "The Big Muddy." On June 2, 1805, they reached the mouth of the Marias River. Here they were faced with trying to decide which flow was the Missouri. A foray up the Marias by Lewis answered the question. Clark in the meantime followed the other waterway and found the "great falls of the Missouri" that the Indians had told them to look for.

The explorers exited the present day National Monument area on June 13, 1805 after having camped about eight miles downstream from the future site of Fort Benton.

Calculations in their journals of latitude and longitude have made it possible to ascertain the approximate location of certain campsites, but others have been altered by the flow of the Missouri.

. . . *homesteaders*

followed their dreams to this wild land,

but found only temporary success.

▲ This cabin was
built in 1918 by
George Middleton,
a crusty old loner
who lived off the
land and the river.
RICK AND SUSIE GRAETZ

The Virgelle
Ferry (mile 39).
RICK AND SUSIE GRAETZ

At least eleven of them are now under the waters of Fort Peck Lake. To experience the entire route, one would have to travel on the river or ride horseback.

The best companion for becoming acquainted with the Lewis and Clark Expedition, is a copy of their journals and *Undaunted Courage*, a masterpiece of writing on the entire adventure by Stephen Ambrose.

In October of 1976, President Gerald Ford signed legislation adding 149 miles of the fabled Upper Missouri River between Fort Benton and Fred Robinson Bridge to the National and Wild and Scenic River System. The reason? "Because it was found to be an irreplaceable legacy of the historic American West." Then, on January 17, 2001, President Bill Clinton gave farther protection to this waterway by declaring the river corridor and 374,976 acres of public land as the National Monument. This new monument is mostly confined to the former Wild and Scenic River corridor as well as farther contiguous breaks country and portions of Arrow Creek, Antelope Creek and the Judith River. State and private lands totaling almost 120,000 acres are also scattered throughout. From Fort Benton to Arrow Creek the protected stretch is mostly limited to the river passageway. From the Arrow Creek drainage to Fred Robinson Bridge, the width varies anywhere from three to 16 miles.

Heading north and east from Fort Benton, the Big River doesn't surge, but rather flows calmly; even the once treacherous rapids such as Deadman's and Dauphine's hardly make a ripple on the surface. Silently passing through fertile river bottoms, it visits some of the west's most remote and least inhabited country. Beautiful rock formations, austere badlands and magnificent river canyon and prairie scenery, coupled with the historical lure of the place, brings floaters back many times over.

The great Indian Nations knew the river first. West of the White Cliffs/Rocks was the homeland of the feared Blackfeet. Below this terrain, the Gros Ventre, Assiniboine and Cree claimed hunting rights. The mountain tribes . . . Kutenai, Salish, Nez Perce, Kalispel and Shoshone—also journeyed here in search of the bison herds.

After Lewis and Clark, owing to strong Indian resistance, whites didn't show up again until 1831, lured, in spite of the dangers, by the monetary rewards of the fur trade. That summer, James Kipp of the American Fur Company, and 25 of his men, established the Blackfeet trading post, Fort Piegan, at the confluence of the Marias and Missouri. Only lasting the winter, it was burned by the Indians and replaced several miles upriver, in the summer of 1832, by Fort McKenzie, named for Kenneth McKenzie of the American Fur Company. This colorful post lasted until 1843 when a foolhearty incident with the Blackfeet Indians caused the place to be abandoned and later burned. The charred remains can still be seen mixed in the cultivated soil of Brulé Bottom, (Brulé means burned in French) the former site of the old fort.

In 1833, a German scientist, Alexander Philip Maximilian, prince of Wied-Neuwied and leader of the North American Scientific Expedition, came to the Upper Missouri to study the Indians and to collect animal and plant specimens. A young Swiss artist, Karl Bodmer, accompanied him. The prince and the painter left Fort Union, at the Montana/North Dakota border, on the keelboat Flora July 6, 1833 and reached Fort McKenzie on August 9 to begin a five-week stay. Enroute, Bodmer performed his magic, showing the world through his paintings what the Upper Missouri River looked like. It's possible today to find most of the actual scenes of Bodmer's 1833 sketches.

Maximilian eloquently described in words the beauty of the river. He recounted ". . . a part of the country called the 'stone walls' has nothing like it on the whole course of the Missouri and we did not leave the deck for a single moment the whole forenoon . . . here, on both sides of the river, the most strange forms are seen, and you may fancy that you see colonnades, small round pillars with large globes or a flat slab at the top, little towers, pulpits, organs with their pipes, fortresses, castles, churches with pointed towers, etc., etc., almost every mountain bearing on its summit some similar structure."

It is interesting to compare Maximilian's thoughts with those of the 1805 visitors. Entering the White Cliffs/Rocks section of the Missouri, Lewis and Clark were so enamored with the sandstone sculptured by time and the elements, that they noted in their journals ". . . the hills and river cliffs, which we pass today exhibit a most romantic appearance . . . eligant ranges of lofty freestone buildings, having their parapets well stocked with statuary . . . seens of visionary inchantment."

In October 1855, near the confluence of the Missouri and Judith rivers a "peace treaty" with many of the Plains Indian tribes was signed. Convened by Isaac Stevens, Governor of Washington Territory, an estimated 3,500 Indians attended (some accounts say 5,000 or more were there). In essence, the agreement stated that the Blackfeet and Gros Ventres would be peaceful when the Nez Perce and Salish crossed the mountains to hunt bison. And the Blackfeet agreed to end hostilities with the Sioux, Assiniboine and Crow. The pact allowed the US Government to use the river and to build roads and military posts. The Indians received gifts and were promised annual annuities. As a result of the council, a Blackfeet Indian agent representing the US was assigned to Fort Benton.

Near the site of this gathering, 11 years later in July 1866, the first military fort in Montana Territory, Camp Cooke, was built. Abandoned in the spring of 1869, its commissary, Fort Clagett, about a mile away on the Missouri, became a civilian trading post. This encampment was the start of the PN Ranch which is still in existence today.

The wild Missouri soon became the lifeline and main "highway" into Montana Territory. All manners of characters used the river, walked its banks and hid out in its canyons and badlands. At first it was used extensively for fur trade by keel boats, dugout canoes and mackinaws, but on July 2, 1860, the steamers Chippewa and Key West reached Fort Benton just prior to the discovery of gold in the Territory. The rush for the glittering metal started in 1862 at Bannack, followed by Alder Gulch (Virginia City) in 1863 and Last Chance Gulch (Helena) in 1864. Folks came to seek their fortune, and steamboats provided the way. During "Benton's" steamboat era, 1860–1890, countless tons of freight and thousands of people made their way through this now protected stretch of geography.

The names of many locations along the river originated in the steamboat days. Landmarks such as Steamboat, LaBarge, Citadel, Pilot Rock and Deadman Rapids were so designated by the big boat captains. And places like Woodhawk Creek were fueling stops for the sternwheelers.

Woodhawks/wolfers, a sometimes double occupation, were an integral part of the river traffic. The steamboats bought logs for fuel from them during the river season and the wolves, or rather their hides, provided income for the winter months when ice closed the passage. Theirs was a dangerous and lonesome life. Scores of "hawkers" were killed, usually by Indians, but often times by the elements. The native people attacked, not only because they didn't want them in their territory, but the poisoned

▸▸ Below Cow Island in the badlands.
RICK AND SUSIE GRAETZ

21

carcasses set to bait wolves, also killed Indian dogs. At times the woodhawks would see their stashes of wood burned by Indians, or perhaps only a fraction of what they cut had sold by the time the season ended. Forgotten piles of wood and old skid trails used to drag the logs to the river edge are still visible.

Apparently this tough breed of men felt the risks were well worth it. Wood could go from $6–$20 a cord depending upon the species of tree and how desperate a captain was for fuel. A boat could burn up to 30 cords of wood in 24 hours (a cord measures 4' x 4' x 8'). As an example, in the spring of 1868 the Steamboat Henry M. Shreve took 67 days to get from St Louis to Fort Benton. During the upriver haul, she burned 1,051 cords of wood at a cost of $6,048. Often, a "hawk" would set up shop by the rapids where the boats had to stop to assess the proper course. Additional fuel was usually needed to get through these rough places, and to the captain's dismay, the prices were often exhorbitant.

Cow Island (mile 126), a landmark along the river, was a low water and late season landing site for steamboats. Here, goods were unloaded and freighted by wagon overland to Fort Benton.

The island was also a major fording spot for Indians and bison. In the fall of 1877, military supplies had been discharged from steamboats. On September 23, 1877, Chief Joseph and the Nez Perce crossed the Missouri here on their historic flight to Canada. After failing to peacefully negotiate for some goods with the small military and civilian contingent guarding it, they took what was needed and burned the rest. An estimated 50 tons of freight was destroyed.

At first, settlers used the steamboats to reach the area, but when the silver spike for the railroad was driven at Fort Benton in the fall of 1887, they made their migration to the Upper Missouri via the steel rails and claimed land along the Missouri's bottom lands.

Three hundred and twenty acres of free ground came to would-be farmers with the Homestead Act of 1909 and the westward rush was on. Along the Missouri after 1910, almost every piece of land with enough level ground to make farming worthwhile had been settled. The drought of 1917–1922, though, combined extreme weather, isolation, and ground unsuitable for farming to force most of the "sod busters" off the land. A few of these dreamers stayed on and are the roots of today's big ranching and farming operations above the canyon rims. Eventually the flow of the water and nature reclaimed much of the abandoned land.

Virgelle, a Homestead Era river town, about 41 miles down from Fort Benton, was founded in 1912 by Virgil and Ella Blankenbaker. At one time the place had a bank, school, post office, grain elevator and general store. The drought and depression years did the town in, although the store operated until 1970. In 1975, Don Sorenson, who grew up near Virgelle, reopened the Mercantile and turned the upstairs into a Bed and Breakfast, filled the old bank with antiques for sale, and fixed up cabins for rent. He has brought a small spark of life back into the town.

The most popular put in place on the river for floaters, Coal Banks Landing about one mile below Virgelle, was another steamboat unloading destination during periods of low water. An attempt by steamboats to use the lignite coal found along the hillsides for fuel didn't work; it would only burn on the edges. Those looking for inexpensive fuel, didn't use it a second time.

Coal deposits found farther downriver from Coal Banks played a role in mining. The owners of the Ruby Gulch Mine in the Little Rockies needing energy to operate their mill, obtained it by developing a coal-fired-steam plant on the Missouri, 23 miles to south of the mine. The facility operated periodically from 1917 to 1923.

"... The hills and river Clifts

which we passed today exhibit a most

romantic appearance."

—L&C May 31, 1805

▲ Last light on
some of the
white rocks.
RICK AND SUSIE GRAETZ

THE RIVER AND BREAKS TODAY

According to the Wild and Scenic River Act, three classifications (recreation, scenic and wild) are assigned to any waterway so designated. Recreation means some development is present and the area is accessed by roads. Scenic has no development, but some places are reached by primitive roads. The wild category translates to no accessibility except by trail. These categories are still valid under Monument status.

From Fort Benton to Coal Banks Landing (mile 42) and beyond to mile 52, the river is classified as recreation. Then from the spectacular White Cliffs/Rocks area for the next 32.5 miles to Deadman's Rapids, the designation is wild. Four miles above and four miles below the popular take out spot at Judith Landing (mile 88.5) is recreation once again. This entire 46.5-mile segment usually takes three days and two nights to float.

Travelers continuing on for three to four more days to the Fred Robinson Bridge (mile 149) pass through additional wild and scenic classifications in a grand, but far less traveled area. A 40-mile stretch of this segment, from Judith Landing to Cow Island, features beautiful badlands, quiet cottonwood stands and reminders of long forgotten homesteads. The last ten miles of designated river are part of the incredible Charles M. Russell National Wildlife Refuge. The CMR, a 1.1 million-acre preserve straddles the free flowing Missouri for another 135 miles of protected landscape, and takes in the 250,000-acre Fort Peck Lake with its 1,600 miles of shoreline, more river breaks and wild prairie grassland.

Three summer-only ferries, one near Loma (mile 20.8), another at Virgelle (mile 41) and the other the Stafford McClelland (near mile 102), provide access across the river from backcountry roads. Only one bridge, the structure at Judith Landing, which connects Big Sandy and Winifred, crosses the entire safeguarded 149-mile span of river; the only way to see the Upper Missouri River Breaks National Monument on the surface is by boat or canoe.

The physical geography of this river country is diverse. Rolling hills, table top rims and fertile bottom lands make up the landscape from Fort Benton to Coal Banks, a myriad of coulees and beautiful rock formations stretch from the Eagle Creek and the White Cliffs/Rocks area on through and past Hole-in-the-Wall, then distinctive badlands, steep slopes and wide banks accent the skyline to Fred Robinson Bridge. Here and there, stands of riverside and island cottonwoods add to the river's beauty.

Relief from the water level to the upper rims varies from 400 feet near Fort Benton to more than 1,000 feet in the badlands and breaks areas below Judith Landing. And depths of the river vary greatly, ranging from a few inches to 15 feet deep.

The White Cliffs/White Rocks country shows some of the most interesting and photogenic scenes on the Upper Missouri. The area's white sandstone crumbles easily while the yellowish-red colored

▸▸ Usually, the

river is tranquil

and peaceful.

RICK AND SUSIE GRAETZ

material found here is harder and therefore more erosion resistant. Thus the white pillars with the tinged caps are formed. Toadstools and thin sand stonewalls, common to this area, were created by wind erosion.

Some of the Monument's farthest downstream reaches are actually a small desert environment. The badlands, or Mauvaises Terres as the French trappers called them, are formed when fire or some other disruption destroys the plant cover that normally protects the soil from being eroded. Rainwater hits the denuded surface compacting it and seeds can't take hold, then runoff forms gullies and soon the strange looking formations appear.

The namesake of the National Monument, the river breaks, are sculptured by the erosive action of water on the soil and soft rocks underlying the surface. Small gulches and deep canyons are cut out of the higher landscape as streams, rainwater and snowmelt find their path to the river. The resulting terrain is rough, wild and spectacular.

Weather patterns along this historic waterway vary widely. Summer can bring searing dry heat with temperatures exceeding 100 degrees, violent thunderstorms, heavy rain, and even hail and snow. In winter, north winds whip up ferocious blizzards and the thermometer may lower to 50 below zero, or warm southwest winds can make a January day feel like spring. May and June, although sometimes wet, bring the beauty of wildflowers and green to the landscape and in late September and October, the gold, orange and red of the shoreline and coulees present a magnificent show against a deep blue and cloudless sky.

Vegetation in this river environment is diverse and includes cottonwood, ash, box elder, willow, pine, juniper, greasewood, cactus, grasses, sagebrush, wild roses, snowberry, wild licorice and low lying riparian growth. Rushes and snake grass found in the wet areas put down a good root system and help hold bank soil in place.

The present lack of cottonwood and willow regeneration on the Missouri is of concern. A truly healthy river is constantly changing as banks and slopes are cut away and rebuilt elsewhere. Silt, carried on the fast high water brought on by uncontrolled runoff from spring floods, is required to prepare seed beds for the air and water borne seeds. Because of upstream dams, this no longer happens. Before the dams, winter water levels were low, hence less ice accumulated. Now in winter, these man-made impediments release more water than before keeping the flow higher, thus allowing a greater amount of damaging ice to build-up. As the ice jams and starts to move, it scours out many of the seedlings that have managed to take hold. Bank beavers are also a threat to cottonwoods.

Hot weather grazing in riparian areas can lead to the destruction of newly sprouted cottonwoods. This is an issue the Bureau of Land Management is attempting to work out with local ranchers. One of the possible solutions is to provide solar powered pumps for water tanks on high ground away from the river. Some operators are voluntarily pulling their stock out of the area during the mid-summer heat. With controls, it is possible for cows and the wild river to successfully co-exist. The Bureau of Land Management (BLM) doesn't want the cattle to disappear from the Monument.

A private organization, Sunburst Unlimited of Great Falls with assistance from US Air Force personnel at Malmstrom Air Base, has planted many cottonwoods in and around the Hole-in-the-Wall campground. The trees seem to be holding their own, thanks to the many floaters who have been gracious enough to pump a pail or two of water for them before heading downstream.

. . . the land remains open to all, as it was

when Lewis and Clark passed this way.

River camp at
Eagle Creek
(mile 55.7).
Lewis and Clark
spent the night
near here on
May 31, 1805.
RICK AND SUSIE GRAETZ

The islands and banks of the Upper Missouri host some unwanted plant-life . . . weeds, especially leafy spurge and Russian knapweed. The BLM has instituted an aggressive program of releasing flea beetles to feast on the leafy spurge. Buck Damone, long-time BLM manager of recreation on the designated waterway and now retired, called the bugs his kids and noted that the millions set free had been making excellent progress. The policy continues as 2,500 to 5,000 beetles, collected from Montana and North Dakota, are released at each monitored site along the river.

Wildlife earn a good living along the banks, coulees and canyons. Sixty species of mammals, 230 types of birds and 20 breeds of amphibians and reptiles make this stretch of the Upper Missouri River and its environs their home. Soft-shelled turtles, beaver and a myriad of waterfowl use the vegetation along the shoreline. This riparian zone is some of the most important habitat in the Breaks. Due to the harsh environment, much of the health and safety of the wildlife depends on it. Mule deer, as well as sharp-tailed grouse, are abundant on the slopes and in the coulees, while the rolling areas above the river bottoms make good territory for antelope and sage grouse. In the CMR National Wildlife Refuge section of the Monument, elk and bighorn sheep are found. Many raptors, including Golden eagles, prairie falcons and hawks, perch and nest in the cliffs above the river. Bald eagles pass through in late fall and early winter.

In these fabled waters, 49 varieties of fish have been identified, including gold-eye, sauger, northern pike, sturgeon and walleye. A segment of the National Monument has one of the six remaining paddlefish populations left in the nation.

The BLM is charged with operating the piece of the Missouri now enjoying National Monument status. Learn what you can about their future plans and offer your input; they are receptive. Your voice will go a long way toward ensuring the river doesn't change from the beautiful place it is today. For more information on the Upper Missouri River Breaks National Monument, including a list of the outfitters, call the Bureau of Land Management in Lewistown at 406-538-7461. The BLM Visitor Center in Fort Benton is also a contact.

▸▸ Returning
from the summit
of Dark Butte
(mile 69.5).
CHUCK HANEY

Paddling past
LaBarge Rock
(mile 56) and
the White Cliffs.
DONNIE SEXTON/
TRAVEL MONTANA

32

▷ From the top of
the White Cliffs
looking across to
the mouth of Eagle
Creek (mile 55.7).
WAYNE MUMFORD

DOWN THE RIVER

This book couldn't have been written without access to the information in the BLM publication, "Upper Missouri National Wild and Scenic River – History Digest." It greatly helped us lay the plan for our work. In an effort to allow you to "see" this wondrous country and experience the adventure as Lewis and Clark and others did, quotes from their journals are printed verbatim; spelling and grammatical errors, warts and all.

A number of landmarks up and down the river served as sign posts for captains and pilots of river boats. Consequently, some of the islands and formations were named after well known river travelers and events arising from boating.

BLM river maps show the Upper Missouri River Breaks National Monument beginning, as mile zero, at Fort Benton, with the mileage increasing as you head downstream. Since modern day floaters prefer to travel with the current, rather than against it as Lewis and Clark initially did, this description moves downriver.

When floating the river, waterproof BLM maps with each river mile marked are available to help determine your position, historical camps, significant landmarks, private land (no camping) and all public land (camping allowed). They can be found in many outdoor shops in Montana or through the Bureau of Land Management, Lewistown District, Airport Road, Lewistown, MT 59457. Ask for the Upper Missouri National Wild and Scenic River Map 1 – 2 and Map 3 – 4. Use these along with the narrative in this book or the Lewis and Clark Journals.

If time allows, the best way to see the Upper Missouri River Breaks National Monument is to climb into a canoe at Fort Benton (mile 0) and paddle on through to Fred Robinson Bridge and the James Kipp Recreation Area, a 149-mile journey. Shorter segments are easily designed to accomodate your schedule.

The pace of the river's flow varies according to the season, amount of rainfall, the releases from upriver dams and weather (strong headwinds definitely slow progress). In the spring, it's often possible to move from five to six miles per hour, while the average mid-summer current is between three and four miles per hour.

Fifteen to 17 miles a day is a good pace; although BLM records show that the average floater travels as much as 22 miles in a day. Most put in at Coal Banks Landing (mile 42) and take out at the Judith Landing Campground (mile 88). This stretch usually takes three days and two nights. For those planning on covering the span from Judith Landing to the Robinson Bridge (mile 149), a distance of 61 miles, it is best to allow three to four days.

Bring plenty of water, a minimum of one gallon per person, per day, because the river water is not drinkable and the very dry, warm air will dehydrate you in a hurry.

Take care when climbing some of the hillsides, as many of them are unstable and slippery. Sandstone is fragile and crumbles easily so watch your footing. And rattlesnakes are present all along parts of the Missouri, so be aware when walking in brushy and rocky areas.

To protect your gear make sure you store it in waterproof containers or "river bags." And extra lashing line to hold your gear in the boat and a spare paddle or two is a good idea. Don't take a chance of overturning and having your equipment float downstream. At night stow your gear away from your boat and tie the craft down for the evening. Pack out what you take in and always leave your campsight in better condition than you found it.

Take these necessary precautions, respect the land and you'll have a great trip. Floating this magnificent scenic river is a great experience you will want to repeat.

Mile 14 – Left Bank – FORT McKENZIE (BRULÉ BOTTOM)

Built late in 1832 to trade with the Piegans, Bloods and Blackfeet, the life of Fort McKenzie was cut short in January of 1844 when a party of young Blackfeet warriors returning from the Crow country asked admittance to the fort and were refused by Francois A. Chardon, a hotheaded Frenchman and his lieutenant, Alexander Harvey. The warriors retaliated by stealing or killing some of the fort's livestock. A well armed party pursued them, but in the fray, Chardon's negro slave was killed and scalped. Vowing revenge, they loaded the fort's cannon with 150 or so lead bullets, aimed it at the approach to the main gate and waited for the next Indian trading party.

In February, a small band of either Piegans or Bloods arrived to trade. Before Harvey could put fire to the cannon, Chardon fired his rifle killing one chief, the other Indians scattered. Only 5 were hit and 2 were killed (although some stories say as many as 30 were killed instantly). Further trading at the fort was impossible. Chardon and company moved downriver to the mouth of the Judith about April 5, 1844. Fort McKenzie was then burned by either whites or Indians, and to this day the site is known as Brulé (burned) Bottom.

Brulé Bottom became the head of navigation for a short time in 1859. A small steamer called the Chippewa reached Brulé Bottom June 17, 1859 and became the first to navigate the Upper Missouri. Short on fuel, concerned by a falling river and being only 12 miles from Fort Benton, Charles P. Chouteau, who was in charge, decided to unload the freight at this point and turn back.

Mile 22 – Left Bank – LEWIS & CLARK CAMP of June 2–11, 1805 and LEWIS RETURN CAMP 1806 – MOUTH OF THE MARIAS RIVER

Commonly called "Decision Point," the area around the confluence of the Marias and the Missouri was the site of many historical events. It was here that as one historian so aptly put it, Lewis and Clark entered the "where the hell are we" phase of their expedition. On the return journey, this is the spot where Lewis rejoined the rest of his contingent after attempting to explore the headwaters of the Marias. Fort Piegan, the first trading post on the Missouri above Fort Union (at the meeting of the Missouri and Yellowstone) was built here in 1831.

34

›› Dark Butte
(mile 66.5).
RICK AND SUSIE GRAETZ

Lewis – Sunday June 2, 1805

"... we came too on the Lard. side in a handsome bottom of small cottonwood timber opposite to the entrance of a very considerable river."

Lewis – Monday June 3, 1805

"This morning early we passed over and formed a camp on the point formed by the junction of the two large rivers . . . An interesting question was now to be determined; which of these rivers was the Missouri . . . to mistake the stream at this period of the season, two months of the traveling season having now elapsed, and to ascend such stream to the rocky Mountain or perhaps much further before we could inform ourselves whether it did approach the Columbia or not, and then be obliged to return and take the other stream would not only loose us the whole of this season but would probably so dishearten the party that it might defeat the expedition altogether. convinced we were that the utmost circumspection and caution was necessary in deciding on the stream to be taken . . . accordingly we dispatched two light canoes with three men in each up those streams; we also sent out several small parties by land with instructions to penetrate the country as far as they conveniently can permitting themselves time to return this evening and indeavour if possible to discover the distant bearing of those rivers by ascending the rising grounds . . . Capt. C. & myself stroled out to the top of the hights in the fork of these rivers from whence we had an extensive and most enchanting view; the country in every derection around us was one vast plain . . . to the South we saw a range of lofty mountains (probably the Highwoods) which we supposed to be a continuation of the S. Mountains (Judiths) . . . behind these Mountains and at a great distance, a second and more lofty range of mountains appeared to stretch across the country in the same direction with the others, reaching from West, to the N of N. W., where their snowey tops lost themselves beneath the horizon. this last range (probably the Little Belts) was perfectly covered with snow. the direction of the rivers could be seen but little way, soon loosing the break of their channels, to our view, in common plain . . . we took the width of the two rivers, found the left hand or S. fork 372 yards and the N. fork 200. The north fork (Marias) is deeper than the other but it's courant not so swift; it's waters run in the same boiling and roling manner which has uniformly characterized the Missouri throughout it's whole course so far; it's waters are of a whitish brown colour very thick and terbid, also characteristic of the Missouri; while the South fork (Missouri) is perfectly transparent runds very rappid but with a smoth unriffled surface it's bottom composed of round and flat smooth stones like most rivers issuing from a mountainous country. the bed of the N. fork composed of some gravel but principally mud; in short the air & character of this river is so precisely that of the missouri below that the party with very few exceptions have already pronounced the N. fork to be the Missouri; myself and Capt. C. not quite so precipitate have not yet decided but if we were to give our opinions I believe we should be in the minority . . . what astonishes us a little is that the Indians who appeared to be so well acquainted with the geography of this country should not have mentioned this river on wright hand if it be not the Missouri; . . . if this right hand or N. fork be the Missouri I am equally astonished at their not mentioning the S. fork which they must have passed in order to get to those large falls which they mention on the Missouri. thus have our cogitating faculties been busily employed all day . . . In the evening the parties whom we had sent out returned . . . Their accounts were by no means satisfactory nor did the information we acquired bring us nigher to the

The variety of weather is part of the

river's personality.

Whitecaps and
headwinds can be
nature's deterrents
to a floater's speed
on the river.
RICK AND SUSIE GRAETZ

The town
of Virgelle
(mile 40.5),
founded in
1912, gives one
an idea of what
life here was
like during the
Homestead Era.
RICK AND SUSIE GRAETZ

decision of our question or determine us which stream to take . . . Capt. C. and myself concluded to set out early the next morning with a small party each, and ascend these rivers untill we could perfectly satisfy ourselves of the one, which it would be most expedient for us to take on our main journey to the Pacific . . ."

Lewis – Tuesday June 4, 1805

"This morning early Capt. C. departed, and at the same time I passed the wright hand fork opposite to our camp below a small Island . . . The north fork which I am now ascending lies to my left and appears to make a considerable bend to the N. W. . . . . I now directed my course through a high level dry open plain. the whole country in fact appears to be one continued plain to the foot of the mountains or as far as the eye can reach . . ."

Lewis – Thursday June 6, 1805

"I now became well convinced that this branch of the Missouri (Marias) had it's direction too much to North for our rout to the Pacific . . ."

Mile 37 – Left Bank – LEWIS & CLARK CAMP of June 1, 1805

After leaving Stonewall Creek (Eagle Creek) that morning, the Corps of Discovery camped in this vicinity, making nearly 19 miles (23 miles by their estimate). They camped on an island, the last in a series of four between here and the Virgelle Ferry crossing. The river shifts a great deal in this area, as the number of gravel bars will attest to, so the exact site is difficult to fix.

Lewis – Saturday June 1, 1805

". . . the river Clifts and bluffs not so high as yesterday and the country becomes more level . . . Capt. C. who walked on shore today informed me that the river hills were much lower than usual and that from the tops of those hills he had a delightfull view of rich level and extensive plains on both sides of the river . . ."

Mile 39 – VIRGELLE FERRY

Provides access from Virgelle to ranching country south of the river.

Mile 43 – Left Bank – COAL BANKS LANDING

Coal Banks is the most popular putting-in spot for floaters heading downriver. Once a steamboat off-loading area, in 1886 it was a military post named Camp Otis. Virgelle, an old homestead town is about one mile upriver on the bench.

Mile 51 – Left Bank – PILOT ROCK (JAPPEY RANCH)

The massive igneous boulder in the ranch yard is commonly known as Pilot Rock. In addition to a captain, most steamboats also carried one or more pilots to guide them safely through the river's channels. These fearless, independant men had nerves of steel and were quick to act on a moments notice.

40

Late afternoon
along the White
Rocks area.
RICK AND SUSIE GRAETZ

Miles 52.2 – 53 Right Bank – EBERSOLE BOTTOM

Jake Ebersole lived here long before the turn of the century. The area was used early in the 1860s as a wood supply yard for steamboats. The remains of several buildings line the riverbanks (this is private land). A structure downriver is a dugout, probably the home of a woodhawk. The coulee mouth in the middle of the sandstone cliff on the left bank is known as The Cove, a popular lunch stop for river floaters.

Mile 53.5 – Right Bank – HORSE RUSTLER'S CABIN

Jimmy or Jack Munro, a squatter in the latter half of the 19th century. Munro, a stone mason by trade, made his living in horses. He never bought or corraled a horse; instead, he let them run wild in the breaks by the hundreds.

Mile 55.7 – Left Bank – LEWIS & CLARK CAMP – May 31, 1805

The Corps of Discovery camped at ". . . the upper part of a timbered bottom on the Stard. side . . . just above the mouth of . . . a stone wall creek (Eagle Creek). Artist Karl Bodmer did many sketches in this scenic area.

Lewis – Friday May 31, 1805

". . . the men are compelled to be in the water even to their armpits, and the water is yet very could . . . added to this the banks and bluffs along which they are obliged to pass are so slippery and the mud so tenacious that they are unable to wear their mockersons, and in that situation draging the heavy burthen of a canoe and walking acasionally for several hundred yards over the sharp fragments of rocks . . . in short their labour is incredibly painfull and great, yet those faithful fellows bear it without a murmur . . . The hills and river Clifts which we passed today exhibit a most romantic appearance. The bluffs of the river rise to the hight of from 2 to 300 feet and in most places nearly perpendicular; they are formed of remarkable white sandstone . . . The water in the course of time in decending from those hills and plains on either side of the river has trickled down the soft sand clifts and woarn it into a thousand grotesque figures, which with the help of a little immagination . . . are made to represent eligant ranges of lofty freestone buildings, having their parapets well stocked with statuary; collumns of various sculpture both grooved and plain, are also seen supporting long galleries in front of those buildings; in other places . . . we see the remains or ruins of eligant buildings . . . the tops of the collumns did not the less remind us of some of those large stone buildings in the U. States . . . as we passed on it seemed as if those seens of visionary inchantment would never have an end; for here it is too that nature presents to the view, of the traveler vast ranges of walls of tolerable workmanship, so perfect indeed are those walls that I should have thought that nature had attempted here to rival the human art of masonry had I not, recollected that she had first began her work . . ."

Mile 55.7 – Left Bank – EAGLE CREEK

In addition to being one of the most scenic locations along the river and a Lewis and Clark campsite, remnants of drive lines, processing stations, tipi rings, rock cairns and flint knapping workshops, reminders of the presence of the area's earliest residents, are found near here. The crew of

The river visits some of the West's most

remote and least inhabited country.

▲ Looking downriver
towards Hole-in-
the-Wall (mile 64).
RICK AND SUSIE GRAETZ

the government boat Mandan was fond of leaving signs of their passing. Their graffiti can still be seen on the river cliffs in several places.

Mile 56 – Right Bank – LABARGE ROCK

This large, dark igneous landmark across the river from Eagle Creek was probably named for Joseph LaBarge, one of the most capable river pilots and a noted steamboat captain.

Mile 56.8 – Left Bank – CASTLE ROCK

A long, sheer, square-cut block of sandstone rising from near the waters edge.

Mile 56.9 – Left Bank – GRAND NATURAL WALL

A thin, fence-like wall of dark rock, runs from the north perpendicular to the water, falling nearly 100 feet to the river's edge. Built up layer upon layer of overlapping blocks of stone, a small portion is visible on the opposite side of the river.

Mile 59.7 – Left Bank – EAGLE ROCK AND KIPP RAPIDS

A spire-like, eagle shaped rock whose head seems to follow your position as you navigate the shoal named for James Kipp who built Fort Piegan, the first trading post in Blackfeet country.

Mile 62 – Right Bank – CITADEL ROCK

Citadel Rock is a State Monument and has been placed on the National Register of Historical Places. Named by early fur traders who used it as a river landmark, it was employed to plot the course of the Lewis and Clark Expedition. Immortalized in a now famous sketch by Karl Bodmer, it serves to emphasize the accuracy and detail which made him famous. The rock inspired Prince Maximilian to write on his downriver voyage of 1833, "... we passed the Citadel Rock, to which we bid adieu for ever, not without regret."

Mile 64 – Right Bank – HOLE-IN-THE-WALL

Hole-in-the-Wall is a large, natural opening high up on a sandstone wall. Accessed by a path leading from the river bank, it is a fairly easy hike to the top. Lt. August V. Kautz, on the Chippewa noted on June 30, 1860, "We passed the Hole in the Wall . . . We were unable to get up the rapids with the Chippewa."

Mile 66.3 – Left Bank – SEVEN SISTERS OR PINNACLES

A large, multi-columned sandstone formation resembling seven rather curvacious figures gathered together.

Mile 69 – Left Bank – STEAMBOAT ROCK

A large sandstone formation on the bluff about one-half mile off of the river, having more or less the shape of a steamboat; it is, according to the Mississippi and Missouri River commissions, 2,215 river miles from St. Louis.

▸ Antelope roam
the flatlands above
the canyon rims.
CHUCK HANEY

Mile 71.2 – Left Bank – LEWIS & CLARK CAMP May 30,1805

Lewis – Thursday May 30, 1805   After a miserable day, making only 5.4 miles. ". . . more rain has now fallen than we have experienced since the 15th of September last. many circumstances indicate our near approach to a country whose climate differs considerably from that in which we have been for many months. the air of the open country is astonishingly dry as well as pure . . ."

Mile 73.2 – PABLO RAPIDS

The treacherous nature of the Upper Missouri was shown when the Marion, commanded by Captain Wolf, went hopelessly aground here in 1866. The entire crew and passengers became so drunk that they were unable to help the boat over the rapids. Another vessel had to be summoned to transfer the freight. Wolf Island, one mile below the top of the rapids, may have been named for the unfortunate captain.

Mile 76.6 – Left Bank – LEWIS & CLARK CAMP of May 29, 1805
and LEWIS RETURN CAMP of July 29, 1806 – SLAUGHTER RIVER

This is one of the few campsites used by the Corps of Discovery on both their outbound and return journeys.

Lewis – Wednesday, May 29, 1805

"today we passed . . . the remains of a vast many mangled carcases of Buffalow which had been driven over a precipice of 120 feet by the Indians and perished; the water appeared to have washed away a part of this immence pile of slaughter and still their remained the fragments of at least a hundred carcases they created a most horrid stench . . . we saw a great many wolves in the neighbourhood of these mangled carcases they were fat and extreemly gentle, Captain C. who was on shore killed one of them with his espontoon. just above this place we came to for dinner opposite the entrance of a bold running river 40 Yds. wide which falls in on Lard. side. this stream we called Slaughter river (Arrow Creek)."

Mile 78.6 – Left Bank – GROS VENTRE INDIAN CAMP

It was from about this vantage point in 1833, looking diagonally across the Missouri up Arrow Creek, that Karl Bodmer painted the Indian encampment.

Prince Maximillian – August 5th, 1833

". . . between considerable hills, on which numbers of Indians had collected. In the front of the eminences the prairie declined gently towards the river where above 260 leather tents of the Indians were set up; the tent of the principal chief was in the fore-ground, and, near it, a high pole, with the American flag. The whole prairie was covered with Indians, in various groups, and with numerous dogs; horses of every colour were grazing round, and horsemen galloping backwards and forwards, among whom was a celebrated chief, who made a good figure on his light bay horse . . ."

Mile 84.5 – DEADMAN RAPIDS

Lewis and Clark deemed this area "Ash Rapids" probably for the few ash trees in the area at the time of their expedition.

An old cabin
at Bullwhacker
Creek in the
badlands
(mile 122.3).
RUSSELL YOUNG

Another account says it honors the men who travelled from the Judith River to Fort McKenzie in 1837, to warn Alexander Culbertson that smallpox had broken out on the boat bringing up trading goods. The Blackfeet refused to believe the men and demanded the wares be brought upriver. On their return to the Judith, one canoe capsized in the rapids and all four men aboard were lost. Their heroic mission was in vain, for within a short time smallpox ravaged the Blackfeet camps.

Mile 86.3 – Right Bank – FORT CLAGETT
Initially a commissary at Camp Cooke in either 1867 or 1868, it continued to supply the area residents until 1882.

Mile 86.8 – Right Bank – CAMP COOKE
The first military outpost in what would become Montana, it was established on July 11, 1866 and abandoned by the army on March 31, 1870.

Mile 88.5 – Left Bank – JUDITH LANDING AND BRIDGE
The Judith Landing Ferry was put into service on August 16, 1887 and crossed the river at mile 87.4. It remained a fixture until the current bridge was finished in the fall of 1982. Floaters can take out or put in here.

Mile 88.9 – Left Bank – LEWIS & CLARK CAMP May 28, 1805
The Corps of Discovery camped here, across from Dog Creek, after traveling 14.5 miles, during which they encountered some of the worst rapids yet.

Lewis – Wednesday May 28, 1805
"Last night we were all allarmed by a large buffaloe Bull, which swam over from the opposite shore and . . . ran up the bank in full speed directly towards the fires, and was within 18 inches of the heads of some of the men who lay sleeping before the centinel could allarm him or make him change his course, still more alarmed, he now took his direction immediately towards our lodge, passing between 4 fires and within a few inches of the heads of one range of the men as they yet lay sleeping, when he came near the tent, my dog (a Newfoundland named Scannon) saved us by causing him to change his course a second time, which he did by turning a little to the right, and was quickly out of sight, leaving us by this time all in an uproar with our guns in our hands, enquiring of each other the cause of the alarm . . ."

". . . This morning we set out . . . and passed a handsome river which discharged itself on the Lard. side . . . it appeared to contain much more water than the Muscle-Shell river, was more rappid but equally navigable . . . the water of this River is clearer much than any we have met . . ." This, the Judith River, at first named "Bighorn" by Lewis, was renamed by Clark in honor of Miss Julia Hancock, who later became his wife.

MILE 101.5 – LEFT BANK – STAFFORD McCLELLAND FERRY
Originating in 1920, a ferry still operates here today.

Mile 102.1 – DAUPHIN RAPIDS

Dauphin Rapids was the worst barrier to navigation on the upper river. As a result, the area was often a beehive of activity as wood fuel was acquired and freight was unloaded, transported overland around the rapids and then reloaded on the boats.

During low water, shoals at Grand (mile 139) and Cow (mile 128) islands meant that steamboats had to be lightened in able to gain clearance. They would unload about half their freight and then fight their way to the bottom of Dauphin Rapids. Here they would unload, and then return for the rest of the goods. Though many boats were severely damaged by the treacherous currents and shallow boulders of Dauphin Rapids, no wrecks were documented.

Mile 103.3 – Right Bank – LEWIS & CLARK CAMP of May 27, 1805

Lewis – Monday May 27, 1805

". . . the bluffs are very high steep rugged, containing considerable quantities of stone and border the river closely on both sides; once perhaps in the course of several miles there will be a few acres of tolerably level land in which two or three impoverished cottonwood trees will be seen . . . the bluffs are composed of irregular tho'horizontal stratas of yellow and brown or black clay, brown and yellowish white sand, of soft yellowish white sandstone and a hard dark brown freestone, also of large round kidney formed and irregular seperate masses of a hard black Iron stone, which is imbeded in the Clay and sand. sorpe little pine spruce and dwarf cedar on the hills. some coal or carbonated wood still makes it's appearance in these bluffs . . ."

Mile 114.2 – Right Bank – LEWIS & CLARK CAMP of May 26, 1805

Lewis – Sunday May 26, 1805

"Set out at an early hour and proceeded principally by the toe line, using the oars mearly to pass the river in order to take advantage of the shores. scarcely any bottoms to the river; the hills high and juting in on both sides, to the river in many places . . . scarcely any timber to be seen except the few scattering pine and spruce which crown the high hills, or in some instances grow along their sides . . . late this evening we passed a very bad rappid which reached quite across the river, (water deep channel narrow graves &c on each side); the party had considerable difficulty in ascending it . . . while they were passing this rappid a female Elk and it's fawn swam down through the waves which ran very high, hence the name of Elk rappids which they instantly gave this place, these are the most considerable rappids which we have yet seen on the missouri . . . opposite to these rappids there is a high bluff and a little above on lard a small cottonwood bottom in which we found sufficient timber for our fires and encampment . . . This is truly a desert barren country . . ."

▸▸ Hole-in-the-Wall

(mile 64).

WAYNE MUMFORD

At Hole-in-the-
Wall (mile 64),
sandstone carved
gargoyles, castle
turrets and spires
ignite the
imagination.
RICK AND SUSIE GRAETZ

Mile 122.3 – Left Bank – CAPTAIN CLARK DISCOVERS THE ROCKY MOUNTAINS May 26, 1805

Clark – Sunday May 26, 1805

". . . from the first sumit of the hill I could plainly see the Mountains on either side which I saw yesterday and at no great distance from me, those on the Stard Side is an errigular range, the two extremeties of which bore West and N. West from me (Bears Paw Mountains). those Mountains on the Lard Side appeared to be several detached Knobs or Mountains riseing from a level open countery (Judith, North Moccasin and South Moccasin mountains), at different distances from me, from South West to South East, on one the most S. Westerly (Snowy Mountains) of those Mountains there appeared to be snow. I crossed a Deep holler and assended a part of the plain elivated much higher than where I first viewed the above Mountains; from this point I beheld the Rocky Mountains for the first time with certainty (today's Little Belt Mountains, an outlier of the Rockies), I could only discover a fiew of the most elivated points above the horizon . . . covered with Snow and the Sun Shown on it in such a manner as to give me a most plain and satisfactory view. whilst I viewed those mountains I felt a secret pleasure in finding myself so near the head of the heretofore conceived boundless Missouri; but when I reflected on the difficulties which this snowey barrier would most probably throw in my way to the Pacific Ocean, and the sufferings and hardships of my self and party in them, it in some measure counterballanced the joy I had felt in the first moments in which I gazed on them; but as I have always held it little Short of criminality to anticipate evils I will allow it to be a good comfortable road untill I am compelled to beleive otherwise."

Mile 126.5 – Left Bank – MOUTH OF COW CREEK – COW ISLAND

Historic Indian and bison crossing and low water steamboat off-loading area. Chief Joseph and the Nez Perce came through here on their epic journey in September 1877. Lewis and Clark passed through on May 26, 1805 and called it Windsor's Creek after one of their party.

Mile 131 – Right Bank – WOODHAWK CREEK

Woodhawk Creek is reminiscent of those woodchoppers who braved the peril of the Indians for the sake of selling their wood at the average price of eight dollars per cord. Their lives were dangerous, and often short.

Mile 132.9 – Right Bank – LEWIS & CLARK CAMP of May 25, 1805

Mile 133 – Left Bank – LEWIS RETURN CAMP of July 30,1806

Heading downriver, the group covered 57 miles from Slaughter River on this day.

Mile 134.1 – Left Bank – OLD POWER PLANT SITE

In 1916, The Ruby Gulch Mine in the Little Rocky Mountains to the north, established a steam-driven electric power plant here for their mill.

Mile 138.9 – Left Bank – HIDEAWAY COULEE

Kid Curry, an outlaw and ally of Butch Cassidy, The Sundance Kid and their Wyoming Hole-in-the-Wall gang, had a hideout five miles up the coulee. Curry, and the Wyoming outlaws held up a train at Wagner, west of Malta, on July 3, 1901. After the robbery, they fled to Curry's hideaway.

Mile 139 – GRAND ISLAND

Here the Upper Missouri River Breaks National Monument and the Charles M. Russell National Wildlife Refuge meet and overlap for the last ten miles .

Mile 146.2 – Right Bank – LEWIS & CLARK CAMP of May 24, 1805

Mile 149 – Right Bank – FRED ROBINSON BRIDGE – JAMES KIPP STATE PARK

This marks the eastern edge of the National Monument. In 1959, the bridge was dedicated to Fred Robinson, an elected official for 40 years, who pushed for a north/south road through Phillips County. The park was named for James Kipp who established the trading post Fort Piegan in 1831.

Chief Joseph and the Nez Perce crossed here at Cow Island (mile 126.5) on their flight to Canada in 1877.
RICK AND SUSIE GRAETZ

▲ Early morning
light silhouettes
the historic bridge
in Fort Benton
(mile 1.2).
RICK AND SUSIE GRAETZ

▸▸ Peace and serenity
Missouri River style.
WAYNE MUMFORD

Visit it! Enjoy it! Cherish and
Protect it!

A natural sand-
stone arch frames
hikers up Neatts
Coulee.
RICK AND SUSIE GRAETZ

The Grand Natural
Wall (mile 56.9).
RICK AND SUSIE GRAETZ

▴ Elk wander the
hillsides in the
CMR portion of
the Monument.
ERWIN AND PEGGY
BAUER

▸▸ In the more
arid, eastern
part of the
National
Monument.
WAYNE MUMFORD

▸ Near Hideaway
Coulee (mile
138.9), home
to the notorious
Kid Curry gang.
RICK AND SUSIE GRAETZ

64

Why protect it?

"Because it is an irreplaceable legacy

of the historic American West."

↟ Rabbit brush
brings a hint of
color to the early
fall landscape.
RICK AND SUSIE GRAETZ

▸▸ Steamboat Rock
(mile 69) lives up
to its name.
RICK AND SUSIE GRAETZ

▴ Downriver
from Coal Banks
Landing.
RICK AND SUSIE GRAETZ

◂ Mushroom
Caprock
(mile 69.5)
near Dark Butte.
CHUCK HANEY

▸ A pastoral
river scene.
WAYNE MUMFORD

To truly experience this *magnificent land,*

one must grab a paddle and get out into the middle of it.

▲ Sunset at
river mile 45.
RICK AND SUSIE GRAETZ

▶▶ Early morning
launch.
DONNIE SEXTON/
TRAVEL MONTANA

▲ Lewis and Clark
were awed by the
bighorn sheep
along the river.
ERWIN AND PEGGY BAUER

◄ Evens Bend
(mile 6.5)
looking upriver
to Fort Benton.
RUSSELL YOUNG

▸ Fall finery
upstream from
Cow Island
(about mile 125).
RICK AND SUSIE GRAETZ

Lunch break,
first day out of
Coal Banks.
RICK AND SUSIE GRAETZ

LaBarge Rock
(mile 56).
RICK AND SUSIE GRAETZ

From Knox
Ridge looking
down on
Kendall Bottoms
(mile 143).
RICK AND SUSIE GRAETZ

▲ The river corridor
is lined with
reminders of the
early settlers.
RICK AND SUSIE GRAETZ

◀◀ Mule deer are
abundant on the
slopes and in
the coulees.
ERWIN AND PEGGY BAUER

▸ Slipping past
the White Cliffs.
CHUCK HANEY

Castle Rock
(mile 56.8).
RICK AND SUSIE GRAETZ

Nearing the end
of the White Rocks
area.
RICK AND SUSIE GRAETZ

We are all entrusted with this *magnificent*

piece of prairie river.

The health of the river and its wildlife

go hand in hand.

▲ The Pelican Patrol,
part of the Missouri
River Air Force.
CHUCK HANEY

▶▶ Near Seven Sisters
(mile 66.3).
RICK AND SUSIE GRAETZ

▲ The Seven Sisters
(mile 66.3).
Count them.
RICK AND SUSIE GRAETZ

◀◀ Exploring a
sandstone funnel.
DONNIE SEXTON/
TRAVEL MONTANA

▸ Ice sheets near
Fort Benton.
CHUCK HANEY

. . . through 1888, an estimated 600 steamboats

plied these amazing waters.

Cool down time,
near Citadel Rock
(mile 62).
RICK AND SUSIE GRAETZ

Farms and ranches
along the river and
rims have deep roots
in the area.
LARRY MAYER

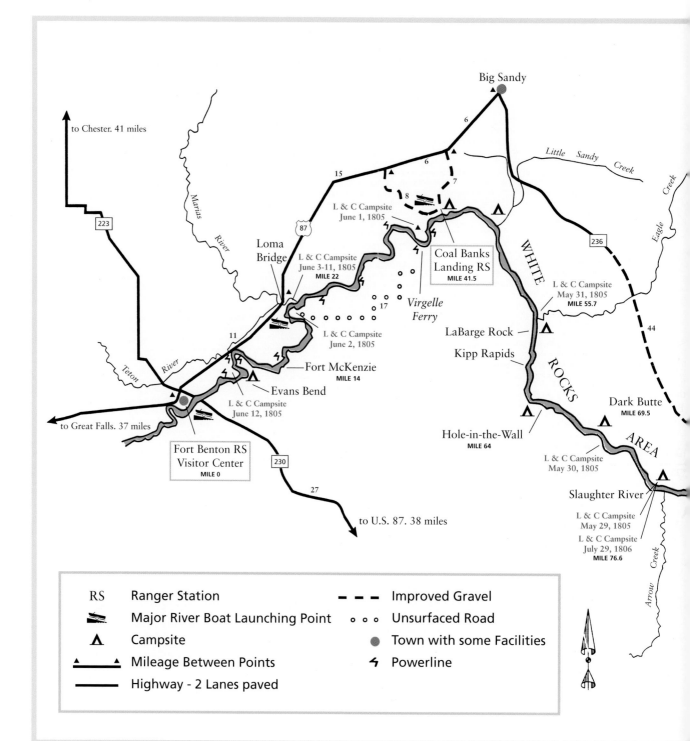

Big Sandy

to Chester. 41 miles

223

87

Marias River

6

15

6

7

8

Little Sandy Creek

Eagle Creek

236

Loma Bridge

L & C Campsite
June 3-11, 1805
MILE 22

L & C Campsite
June 1, 1805

Coal Banks
Landing RS
MILE 41.5

WHITE

17

Virgelle
Ferry

L & C Campsite
May 31, 1805
MILE 55.7

44

LaBarge Rock

11

Kipp Rapids

ROCKS

L & C Campsite
June 2, 1805

Fort McKenzie
MILE 14

Dark Butte
MILE 69.5

Teton River

Evans Bend

Hole-in-the-Wall
MILE 64

AREA

to Great Falls. 37 miles

L & C Campsite
June 12, 1805

L & C Campsite
May 30, 1805

Fort Benton RS
Visitor Center
MILE 0

230

Slaughter River

L & C Campsite
May 29, 1805

L & C Campsite
July 29, 1806
MILE 76.6

27

to U.S. 87. 38 miles

Arrow Creek

RS — Ranger Station	- - - Improved Gravel
Major River Boat Launching Point	o o o Unsurfaced Road
△ Campsite	● Town with some Facilities
▲___▲ Mileage Between Points	⚡ Powerline
Highway - 2 Lanes paved	

94

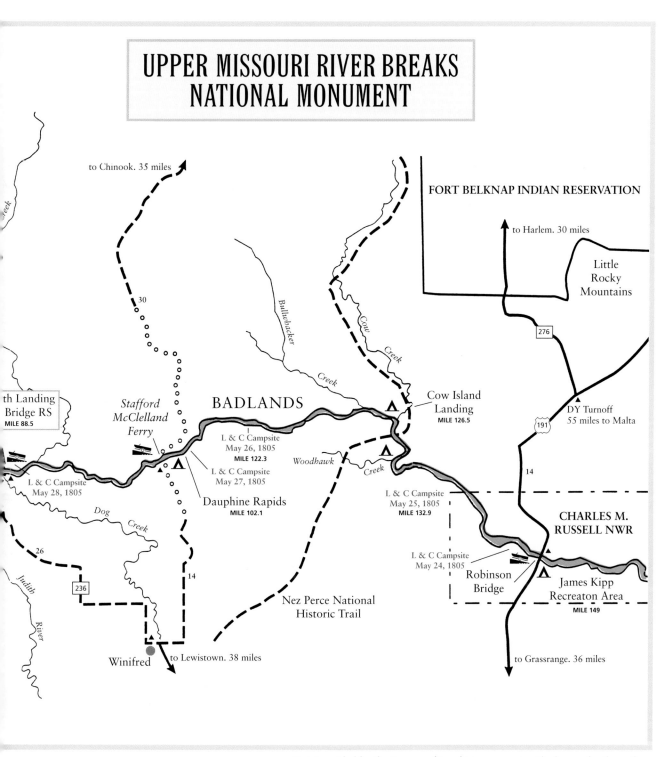

UPPER MISSOURI RIVER BREAKS NATIONAL MONUMENT

FORT BELKNAP INDIAN RESERVATION

to Chinook. 35 miles

to Harlem. 30 miles

Little Rocky Mountains

276

30

Bullwhacker

Cow Creek

Creek

th Landing Bridge RS
MILE 88.5

Stafford McClelland Ferry

BADLANDS

Cow Island Landing
MILE 126.5

DY Turnoff
55 miles to Malta

191

L & C Campsite
May 26, 1805
MILE 122.3

Woodhawk

14

L & C Campsite
May 28, 1805

L & C Campsite
May 27, 1805

L & C Campsite
May 25, 1805
MILE 132.9

CHARLES M.
RUSSELL NWR

Creek

Dog

Dauphine Rapids
MILE 102.1

Creek

26

L & C Campsite
May 24, 1805

Robinson Bridge

James Kipp Recreaton Area
MILE 149

Judith

236

14

Nez Perce National Historic Trail

River

Winifred

to Lewistown. 38 miles

to Grassrange. 36 miles

95

Map provided by the Bureau of Land Management with changes by the author.

Each day on the
river presents
provoking scenery.
Near river mile 66.
RICK AND SUSIE GRAETZ